FIRST NATIONS OF NORTH AMERICA

# SOUTHEAST INDIANS

ANDREW SANTELLA

HEINEMANN LIBRARY
CHICAGO, ILLINOIS

**www.heinemannraintree.com**
Visit our website to find out
more information about
Heinemann-Raintree books.

**To order:**

☎ Phone 888-454-2279

🖥 Visit www.heinemannraintree.com
to browse our catalog and order online.

Original illustrations © Capstone Global Library, Ltd., 2012
Illustrated by Mapping Specialists, Ltd.
Originated by Capstone Global Library, Ltd.
Printed by China Translation and Printing Company

15 14 13 12 11
11 10 9 8 7 6 5 4 3 2 1

**Library of Congress Cataloging-in-Publication Data**
Santella, Andrew.

Southeast Indians / Andrew Santella.

p. cm.—(First nations of North America)

Includes bibliographical references and index.

ISBN 978-1-4329-4952-5 (hc)—
ISBN 978-1-4329-4963-1 (pb) 1. Indians of North America—
Southern States—Juvenile literature. I. Title.

E78.S65S26 2012

975.004'97—dc22          2010042641

**Acknowledgments**

The author and publisher are grateful to the following for
permission to reproduce copyright material:

Alamy: pp. 9 (© North Wind Picture Archives), 23 (© David
Lyons); Corbis: p. 41 (© Christopher Felver); Getty Images: pp.
5 (Nativestock.com/Marilyn Angel Wynn), 14 (Evans/Three
Lions/ MPI), 17 (Willard R. Culver/National Geographic), 27
(Hulton Archive), 29 (MPI), 31 (Nativestock.com/Marilyn
Angel Wynn), 32 (Hulton Archive), 33 (MPI), 40 (STAN
HONDA/AFP); Library of Congress Prints and Photographs:
pp. 16, 18, 26, 34, 39; Nativestock.com: pp. 15 (© Marilyn
Angel Wynn), 19 (© Marilyn Angel Wynn), 20 (© Marilyn
Angel Wynn), 21 (© Marilyn Angel Wynn), 22 (© Marilyn
Angel Wynn), 25 (© Marilyn Angel Wynn), 28 (© Marilyn
Angel Wynn), 30 (© Marilyn Angel Wynn), 35 (© Marilyn
Angel Wynn), 37 (© Marilyn Angel Wynn); Shutterstock:
pp. 8 (© Dean Pennala), 13 (© Anne Kitzman); The Granger
Collection, NYC: 12.

Cover photograph of a mask created by Dan Morse (Lelooska)
Smith of Cherokee origin reproduced with permission from
the National Museum of the American Indian (Smithsonian
Institution/Walter Larrimore/ D2D261527).

We would like to thank Dr. Scott Stevens for his invaluable
help in the preparation of this book.

Every effort has been made to contact copyright holders of
any material reproduced in this book. Any omissions will
be rectified in subsequent printings if notice is given to
the publisher.

# Contents

Some words are shown in bold **like this**. You can find out what they mean by looking in the glossary.

# Who Were the First People in North America?

In 1838 an American Indian man named George Hicks prepared to leave his home in Tennessee. Hicks was leading a group of his Cherokee people hundreds of miles west to new homes in what was then called **Indian Territory**, which is present-day Oklahoma. They had been ordered to move by the U.S. government. It was a painful time for Hicks and his people. He wrote: "We are now about to take our final leave and kind farewell to our native land, the country that the Great Spirit gave our Fathers."

Long before Europeans arrived in North America, native peoples there developed many rich, varied **cultures**. This book tells the story of the American Indians who made their homes in what is now the southeastern United States. Like Hicks, many had to endure the pain of being driven from their homes. But today their **descendants** proudly carry on their history.

▲ A young Cherokee grass dancer performs at a festival.

◄ This Seminole boy is wearing traditional **patchwork** clothing.

## American Indian or Native American?

Sometimes the native peoples of North America are referred to as American Indians. Sometimes they are called Native Americans. So which is correct? When Italian explorer Christopher Columbus came to the Americas in 1492, he used the name "indios", or "Indians", to describe the native peoples. This was because he mistakenly believed he was in the Indies—an old term for Asia. "Native American" came into use in the 1960s, as an alternative to "Indian."

Today, the descendants of the first people to live in North America would say that either term is acceptable. Better still, most would prefer to be identified by their unique group, called a **nation** or **tribe**—for example, "I'm a Cherokee."

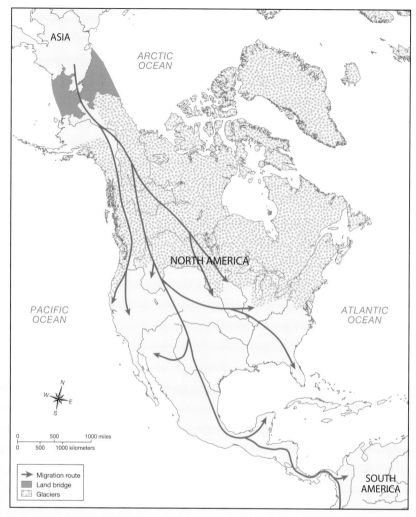

◄ This map shows some of the routes early peoples took as they spread across North America.

## Migrating to America

People have lived in North America for at least 12,000 years. Scientists believe that people **migrated** there by walking across a land bridge that once linked North America to Asia. Then, over many years, they spread out across North and South America. They developed new skills and new ways of life to suit the different **environments** in which they settled.

## Culture areas

Experts who study American Indians divide North America into 10 **culture areas**. Each culture area has its own distinctive **geography**, **climate**, and ways of life. Before European explorers arrived, as many as several million Indians thrived across North America.

◀ This map shows the 10 American Indian culture areas of North America.

# Early peoples of the Southeast

The Southeast culture area stretches from present-day Virginia to the Gulf of Mexico, and from the Atlantic Ocean to present-day Louisiana. It includes what are now the states of Tennessee, North Carolina, South Carolina, Georgia, Florida, Alabama, Mississippi, and Louisiana. More early peoples lived in the Southeast culture area than in many other parts of native North America.

The earliest peoples who lived in the Southeast left no written records. Everything we know about them is based on the objects they left behind. At places like Dust Cave, in Alabama, **archaeologists** have found stone tools and weapons made by some of the first peoples to live in the region—about 11,000 years ago.

▲ The Smoky Mountains are part of the Southeast.

## Adapting to the environment

Early native peoples found a rich natural environment in what is now the southeastern United States. They enjoyed a mild climate with plentiful rainfall. The geography ranged from low-lying swamps to forested hills to tall mountains.

The first peoples of the Southeast lived a **nomadic** life. They moved from place to place, hunting animals and gathering wild plants. Hunters pursued many wild animals, ranging from squirrels and rabbits to bison and bears. Tribes that lived along rivers, lakes, or the Atlantic coast could depend on many kinds of fish, as well as animals such as turtles, as sources of food. Forests provided timber and other raw materials for building homes.

# Agriculture

After several thousand years, people in the region began to pursue **agriculture**. They began raising corn, and they settled in villages along rivers. In many parts of the region, the rich soil was perfect for farming. Farming became the main occupation for many tribes of the Southeast, although they also hunted, fished, and gathered wild plants.

ART AND CULTURE

## Mound Building

Around 3,000 years ago, early Southeast peoples began building huge mounds used for religious **ceremonies**. No one is sure what happened to these Mound Builders. By the time Europeans arrived in the 1500s, the mound construction was slowing down. By 1700 the tradition of mound building had ended. The Southeast Indians we know today may be descendants of the Mound Builders.

▲ Saul's Mound in Tennessee was one of many mounds built for religious ceremonies by early Southeast Indians.

## Diverse nations

The mountains, valleys, and **plains** of the Southeast supported many different tribes:

In the highlands around the Smoky Mountains lived the Cherokee. They were one of the largest Indian groups in the region.

In the foothills to the east lived the Catawba. They were famed for their battles with invading tribes from the north.

▲ This map shows some of the traditional **tribal** homelands of the Southeast.

## Indian Place Names

Traces of Southeast Indian languages are found in the names of many cities, states, rivers, and lakes in the United States. Tennessee gets its name from a major Cherokee town called Tanasi. Alabama is named for the Alabama peoples, a tribe of the Creek Confederacy. Sarasota, a city in Florida, gets its name from a Calusa word meaning "point of rocks."

The plains of Georgia and Alabama were home to the Creek Confederacy. The Muscogee people made up the core of the confederacy, which also included the Hitchiti, Yamasee, Yuchi, and other tribes.

Northern Florida was dominated by the Apalachee and Timucua.

Southern Florida was home to the Calusa people. They were ruled by king-like **chiefs**.

In the 1700s, a group that became known as the Seminole migrated to Florida from Georgia and Alabama.

The Choctaw lived in dozens of towns across what is now Mississippi and parts of Louisiana and Alabama.

To the north along the Mississippi River lived the Chickasaw. They were known for their military skills.

Also along the Mississippi were the Natchez people. Their culture resembled that of the ancient Mound Builders.

# How Did Early Southeast Indians Survive?

As we have seen, Southeast Indians lived in an **environment** well-suited to **agriculture**. **Fertile** soil and plentiful rainfall allowed them to raise a variety of crops. Farming became the main source of food for many **tribes** of the Southeast.

Farmwork began in the early spring, when people burned the fields to prepare them for planting. This cleared away small plants and the remains of old crops. The resulting ash acted as a **fertilizer**, returning rich **nutrients** to the soil.

▲ This drawing from 1591 shows Southeast Indians planting crops.

Farmers first turned the soil over with hoes made of bone and wood. They then used digging sticks to create holes, where they placed seeds. Once the crops were planted, women took over the task of tending the fields. Children were taught to guard the fields, chasing away birds and small animals that tried to eat the crops.

## Crops

Corn was the most important crop for most tribes. It grew well in many areas, was easily stored, and could be prepared in a variety of ways. Corn was almost always planted alongside squash and beans. Cornstalks provided a pole for bean vines to climb. The leaves of the squash plants helped keep the soil moist. Because the three crops worked so well together, they were often called the Three Sisters. Other crops included sweet potatoes, peas, onions, and cabbages. Southeast Indians also gathered wild grapes, strawberries, hickory nuts, and many other fruits and vegetables.

▲ Corn was a basic food for Southeast Indians.

▲ This engraving from 1564 shows Southeast Indian hunters using their skill to approach deer.

## Hunting

Although farming was the main occupation for many early Southeast Indians, hunting was also an important source of food. Hunters pursued large animals, such as deer and bears, as well as smaller **game**, such as rabbits, squirrels, turkeys, and quail.

These animals provided much more than just meat. Early Southeast Indians used the skins and furs of animals to make clothes, robes, and bedding. They also used the bones of animals to make tools.

Hunting was especially important in the fall. During this season, hunters tried to provide enough meat and animal skins to keep their people comfortable through the winter. Hunting was so important that tribes developed customs that they believed would ensure a successful hunt. Hunters often **fasted** and prayed before going on a hunt. A hunter who killed an animal would pray for forgiveness from the animal's spirit.

## Tools and weapons

Before they acquired guns, early Southeast Indians used bows and arrows to hunt deer and other large game. Sometimes hunters disguised themselves in deerskins and antlers so that they could creep up close to animals without alarming them. They caught smaller animals such as rabbits in traps and then killed them with clubs.

One distinctive weapon of the Southeast was the blowgun. A hunter could fire sharp, poisoned darts at a target by propelling it through a long, hollow piece of river **cane** with his breath.

▲ River cane blowguns and darts like these were used by the Choctaw and other early Southeast peoples to hunt small game.

▲ Fishing with spears worked well in Florida's shallow waterways.

## Fishing

For Southeast Indian peoples who lived near bodies of water, fish were an important food source. On the Mississippi River, the Natchez people caught eels and catfish. In the Gulf of Mexico, the Timucua and Biloxi fished for grouper, flounder, and other saltwater fish. Further inland, the Choctaw and Chickasaw found freshwater fish like bass or perch.

Southeast Indians fished with hooks, nets, spears, and bows and arrows. To catch fish in shallow water, they sometimes used a **weir**—a kind of trap set up underwater. Some tribes made a poisonous powder from ground roots and herbs. Sprinkled on water, the powder would paralyze fish so that they could be easily caught.

Fishing was especially important for the Calusa people of Florida. Unlike other tribes, they did not farm. They depended on the fish and other animals they found in bays and rivers. Calusa women caught shellfish such as crabs, lobsters, and oysters. They used seashells to make tools, weapons, and jewelry.

## Dugout canoes

Rivers were natural highways for the early Southeast Indians. Traveling by water was often much easier and faster than traveling by foot through forests, swamps, and marshes. One of the major methods of transportation was the dugout **canoe**. The Calusa and other tribes made these canoes from the trunks of poplar or cypress trees. The Calusa were said to have used their canoes to travel as far away as Cuba.

◄ Dugout canoes allowed Southeast Indians to cover long distances by water.

# What Were Early Southeast Indian Villages Like?

Early Southeast Indians lived in highly organized villages or towns. Their villages were usually established along rivers. These rivers connected them to other communities. The villages were often surrounded by fences called **stockades**. These offered protection from enemies.

In the center of town was a **plaza**. Here, the community gathered for special occasions. The town council met in a council house in the central plaza of Southeast Indian towns. The Cherokee and other groups kept **sacred** fires burning in their central plazas (see page 31). The Natchez people built temple mounds at the center of their towns. Surrounding the central plaza were family homes and small gardens. Around the edge of each town were large farm fields.

◄ This sketch from the 1500s shows a Southeast Indians village surrounded by a stockade.

▲ Some Southeast Indians still play the traditional game of stickball.

The Choctaw, Creek, and Cherokee peoples divided their communities into "red towns" and "white towns." Red towns were devoted to war and were home to the **tribe's** battle leaders. White towns promoted peaceful relations and were home to the tribe's peacetime leaders.

## "Little brother of war"

Most Southeast tribes played a game called stickball. Players used wooden sticks with loops on one end to throw a ball through an opposing team's goal. Games were sometimes staged to resolve disputes between rival towns or tribes. Some games involved more than 100 players on each team. Play could become violent. It is no wonder stickball was called the little brother of war.

## Homes

Early Southeast Indians used the natural materials they found around them to build their houses. Grasses, reeds, river **cane**, tree bark, and wood all went into their homes. Houses were designed to suit the **climate**. In the mountains and on the interior **plains**, tribes had to deal with warm summers and cold winters.

The Cherokee, Creek, and other tribes in these areas used separate houses for summer and winter. Summer houses were large, airy, and designed to keep families cool in the heat of summer. Winter houses were smaller and had no windows. They were lined with clay to keep in the heat of the family fire.

▲ Houses like this Cherokee **wattle-and-daub** structure suited the local climate and **environment**.

▲ This Seminole chickee is open to cooling breezes.

## Wattle and daub

The most common building style was called wattle and daub. These houses were made of bark, vines, and river cane woven into a frame of wooden poles. The walls were lined with plaster made from mud or clay.

After the arrival of non-Indian settlers, some Indians took to living in log cabins and other European-style houses.

## Chickees

One of the most distinctive houses of the Southeast Indians was the Seminole **chickee**, a wall-less house on stilts. Thick wooden posts supported a raised floor. The structure was topped by a roof made of grasses or the leaves of the palmetto tree. The chickee kept families cool in the steamy heat of Florida. Because it was above ground, snakes and other animals could not get into the house.

# What Were Early Southeast Indian Families Like?

Early Southeast Indian families included not just parents and children, but also grandparents, aunts, uncles, and cousins. All worked together to support each other. Aunts, uncles, and grandparents helped parents educate and raise their children.

## Clans

Family members were also part of larger units called **clans**. A clan is a group of people who share a common **ancestor**, or family member from the distant past. Members of the same clan consider themselves to be closely related.

▲ Early Southeast Indian families included extended family members like aunts, uncles, and cousins.

Membership in a Southeast Indian clan was usually passed on through mothers. Rules forbid people from marrying someone from the same clan. When a husband and wife had children, their children belonged to the mother's clan.

Early Southeast Indians were expected to obey the rules of their clan and to help clan members who were in need. When a crime was committed, the victim's clan would seek justice against any member of the wrongdoer's clan.

## Clan totems

Many Southeast Indian clans are named for animals. **Tribes** of the Creek Confederacy divided into nearly 50 different clans, including Bear, Eagle, and Alligator. Timucua clans included Quail, Buzzard, and Fish. These animals served as symbols or **totems** of the clan. Each clan highly prized its totem. The clan totem was believed to serve as a guardian spirit that would protect clan members.

▲ Early Southeast Indians created totems similar to this one that was created by a modern artist.

## Family roles

Each member of a Southeast Indian family had a part to play in supporting the family and the community. Women tended crops in the family garden and in the community fields. They prepared and preserved food, and they made clothing and blankets. They wove baskets and made clay pots for storing food and other items. Among the Choctaw, Cherokee, and other tribes, women were often recognized as powerful leaders of the community. Southeast Indians continue many of these traditions today.

Men provided food by hunting and fishing, and they defended their communities from attacks from other peoples. They made tools and weapons, and they built homes. Men led their communities as **chiefs** and members of councils.

By the time they turned three or four years old, children began learning the skills they would need as adults. Girls learned about cooking and crafts from their mothers. They also helped their mothers tend farm fields. Boys prepared to become warriors and hunters. They played ball games and shot at targets with bows and arrows.

### A DAY IN THE LIFE OF AN EARLY CREEK CHILD

If you were a child among the early Creek people, you were expected to help with chores. On a typical warm, summer day, girls would pick wild berries or tend small gardens. Boys would hunt small animals with spears or bows and arrows. If a boy was skilled enough to make a killing, his proud family would prepare a meal with the meat and offer it as a present to the town's leaders.

▲ These Seminole women are using a hollow log and a wooden stick to grind corn.

# How Did Early Southeast Indians Dress?

The clothes of early Southeast Indians did more than just protect them from the weather. The clothes people wore could also help identify them as members of a particular **tribe**. For example, the Yuchi decorated their clothes with beads set in patterns to look like moons, stars, and animals. Other tribes developed their own distinctive styles of clothing. The Seminole and Miccosukee are famous for their brightly colored **patchwork** shirts.

Some clothing styles were common across the region. Men in most tribes wore garments called **breechcloths** that covered them below the waist. In cool weather, they would add leggings made of deerskins and robes or capes of animal skins. Women wore shawls and wraparound skirts made of deerskins or woven from the bark of mulberry trees. Beginning in the 1800s, tribes adopted some European styles of dress.

▲ This lithograph from 1842 shows a Seminole wearing red leggings.

## Personal appearance

Early Southeast Indians often decorated their bodies with tattoos and face paint. Both men and women wore tattoos created with sharp objects such as stone, bone, or shell dipped in dark dye. Many people pierced various body parts so they could wear jewelry and ornaments.

Choctaw people found wide, flat foreheads attractive. They therefore developed a technique to achieve this effect. They placed small bags of sand or pieces of wood on the foreheads of their sleeping infants. Over time, the weight gently and painlessly flattened the baby's forehead.

▲ Southeast Indians such as this Cherokee leader sometimes decorated their bodies with tattoos and face paint.

# What Objects Did Early Southeast Indians Make?

Early Southeast Indians made everyday objects such as pots and baskets with great skill and care. The Chitimacha people of Louisiana made **cane** baskets by dyeing strips of river cane different colors, then weaving them into complex patterns. The colorful dyes were created by boiling roots and plants that grew in the area. Seminole women used wild grasses they found growing in the Everglades to make their baskets.

▲ Modern Cherokee potters make vases, pipes, bowls, and other beautiful objects.

The Catawba people of the Carolinas used clay they dug from pits along rivers to make their distinctive pottery. First, the clay had to be carefully worked into the desired shape. Then, the pottery would be baked in an open fire to harden and color the clay. Today, many Southeast Indian artists continue to use traditional techniques to make beautiful objects.

## Calusa Wood Carvings

The powerful Calusa people lived in what today is southern Florida. Much of what we know about them comes from objects found by **archaeologists**. In the 1890s, archaeologists on Marco Island in Florida found hundreds of statues, masks, and other Calusa wood carvings buried in mud. The mud had helped preserve the works of art for hundreds of years. Many of the carvings were figures of animals, including pelicans, alligators, and sea turtles. One of the most famous of the carvings, known as the Key Marco Cat, is a 6-inch (15-centimeter) statue of a panther. It is now part of the collection of the Smithsonian Institution in Washington, D.C.

▶ Carvings such as this cat by the Calusa people are more than 1,000 years old.

# What Beliefs Did Early Southeast Indians Have?

Early Southeast Indians believed they were closely linked to the plants, animals, and other beings in the world around them. It was very important to them to maintain harmony with the natural world and with other people. Even everyday actions such as hunting and planting had spiritual meaning. They believed that living with respect for nature and for other people would strengthen their connection to the spirits and gods.

▲ This contemporary painting shows a Seminole Green Corn **Ceremony**. Lasting sometimes as long as eight days, the celebration involved stomp dancing, **fasting**, and other rituals honoring renewal and thanksgiving.

▲ The Eternal Flame at Red Clay State Park in Tennessee memorializes all who died on the Trail of Tears and symbolizes the continuation of Cherokee **culture** today.

Some **tribes** regarded the Sun as the source of life. They believed that their people were **descendants** of the Sun—for example, the Yuchi called themselves children of the Sun. The **chief** of the Natchez people was called the Great Sun. In the central **plaza** of their towns, many other tribes kept a **sacred** flame burning, which represented the Sun.

## The Green Corn Ceremony

The most important of the annual events of the Southeast Indians was the Green Corn Ceremony. Each tribe performed a slightly different version of the celebration. But the main purpose was to give thanks for the gifts of nature and to celebrate the new harvest. The Green Corn Ceremony was also a time for new beginnings. People replaced old or broken belongings and forgave past crimes. The sacred fire was put out. It was then relit to purify it and make it new. Many modern members of Southeast Indian tribes still observe elements of this ceremony.

# When Did Southeast Indians First Meet Non-Indians?

The first Europeans to encounter Southeast Indians were members of an **expedition** led by Spanish explorer Juan Ponce de León. The meeting was not a peaceful one. Ponce de León had come to Florida in 1513 looking for riches and treasure. Failing to find them, he decided to take slaves. Calusa warriors fought a long battle against Ponce de León and his Spanish soldiers. It was the first violence between Europeans and American Indians. Because of the conflict, Ponce de León and his troups left Florida. When he returned eight years later, he was killed by a Calusa arrow.

▲ Legend says Ponce de León came to North American in search of the Fountain of Youth, a mythical spring that restored youth to anyone who drank its waters.

▲ This old woodcut shows Hernando de Soto's Spanish soliders attacking a village of Florida Indians. Torture methods included cutting off various body parts such as hands and nostrils.

Beginning in 1539, a Spaniard named Hernando de Soto led an army through the Southeast. The Spanish encountered the Chickasaw, Cherokee, Creek, and other **tribes**. When Indians tried to defend themselves against the advancing army, the Spanish burned their villages and killed many of them. By 1565 the Spanish had established a settlement at St. Augustine, in what became Florida. Before long, French and English settlers followed the Spanish into North America.

The Europeans brought with them tools and weapons that changed American Indian life. By trading with the Europeans, Indians acquired guns, steel hatchets, kettles, and cloth. But the Europeans also brought with them diseases that killed thousands of American Indians. Tribes such as the Calusa were almost wiped out by the violence and disease that came with the arrival of Europeans in North America.

## Sequoyah's Written Language

Like other Indian languages, Cherokee language existed only in spoken form. Cherokees did not have a written form of their language. A Cherokee named Sequoyah (about 1760-1843) changed all that. He invented a Cherokee **syllabary**, or system of writing. In 1821 the Cherokee council of leaders made it the official Cherokee written language. Soon thousands of Cherokee were learning to write in their own language. In 1828 the *Cherokee Phoenix* began to be published, using the system that Sequoyah invented.

▲ Sequoyah was a silversmith by trade. The *Cherokee Phoenix* was the first newspaper for American Indians by American Indians.

## Resistance

Tribes of the Southeast formed **alliances** with the European countries seeking control of North America. For example, the Choctaws became allies of the French, while the Chickasaws joined forces with the English. But European powers were driven out of most of the Southeast after the Revolutionary War (1775–1783), when the United States became an independent country.

The young United States grew rapidly. Hungry for land, settlers pushed into areas that tribes of the Southeast had long called home. Tribes fought fiercely to protect themselves. In 1813 a group of Creeks battled U.S. soldiers in Alabama. They were eventually defeated and forced to give up much of their homeland.

▲ This early sketch from about 1813 shows Creek warriors defending their village against U.S. troops.

In Florida during the 1800s, the Seminole people fought a long war against U.S. expansion. The Seminole included people from the Hitchiti, Yuchi, Creek, and Yamasee tribes.

## Adapting

Even as fighting continued, many tribes adopted the ways of the settlers. They began raising farm animals and growing wheat. Some gave up traditional Indian houses for log cabins. Others converted to **Christianity**. The Cherokee people even developed a system of government with a constitution modeled after that of the United States.

# Why Did Southeast Indians Have to Leave Their Homes?

Southeast Indians could not stop the flow of non-Indian settlers into their homelands. Instead, U.S. president Andrew Jackson decided that the Indians would have to leave the Southeast. In 1830 he signed into law the Indian Removal Act. This law allowed the United States to move Indians to new homes west of the Mississippi River.

Cherokee leaders fought against such unfair laws in the U.S. courts. But Jackson was determined to move the **tribes** to **Indian Territory** (present-day Oklahoma). Leaders of various tribes signed **treaties** agreeing to the move—but they, in fact, had little choice.

▶ This map shows routes Southeast Indians took to Indian Territory.

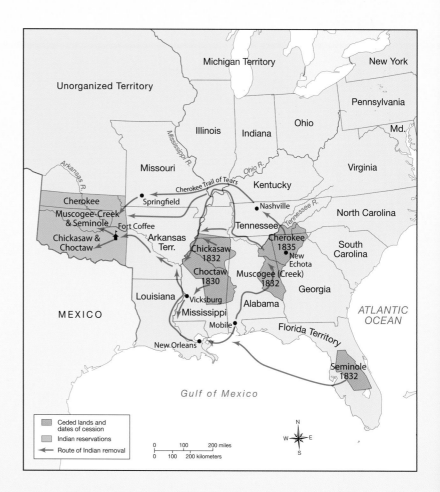

▲ Some 15,000 Cherokee moved west on the Trail of Tears. This painting, by a contemporary Cherokee artist, depicts one of the most tragic events in U.S. history.

## The Trail of Tears

The Choctaw began moving west in 1831. Traveling by foot over hundreds of miles, many suffered from lack of supplies and food. Other Choctaw people stayed in Mississippi, but were often cheated out of their land by settlers.

One by one, other tribes **migrated** west. Groups of Creek and Seminole Indians fought bitterly against the move. Some remained in their homes in Alabama and Florida, but most eventually moved. In 1838 U.S. troops began imprisoning thousands of Cherokee in **stockades**. They were forced west on foot, by wagon, and in boats, while settlers took all their belongings. Cold, hunger, and disease killed many on the long journey. More than 4,000 American Indians died. The trip became known as the Trail of Tears.

# Rebuilding

The tribes that moved to Indian Territory worked to rebuild communities in their new homes. They had to adapt to strange, new **environments**. Each tribe was assigned to live in a portion of Indian Territory. But these new lands were sometimes very different from the homes they had left behind. The Cherokee settled along the Arkansas River in Indian Territory, the same way they had built villages near the rivers of the Southeast.

Though there were differences, the tribes were able to adapt. They established **tribal** governments. They built schools. Some even dreamed of creating an all-Indian state to be named Sequoyah, after the inventor of the Cherokee **syllabary** (see page 35).

▲ This map shows where Southeast Indians made new homes in Indian Territory.

▲ The land rush resulted in thousands of new non-Indian settlers moving into the area that would become the state of Oklahoma.

But once more, non-Indian settlers became greedy for tribal lands. Land that had been promised to the tribes was opened up to non-Indian settlers. Millions of acres of this land were sold. In 1887 the U.S. Congress passed the Dawes Act, which did away with tribal claims to land. Instead, land was assigned to individuals. By 1907 Oklahoma had become a state, and the Indian Territory had ceased to exist. Indians made up just over 5 percent of the new state's population.

# What Is Modern Life Like for Southeast Indians?

In the 1900s, American Indians gained more rights. In 1924 the Congress passed the Indian Citizenship Act. This made all Indians citizens of the United States. The Indian Reorganization Act of 1934 tried to give American Indians more control over their lives. It allowed them to practice traditional **ceremonies**.

Not every Southeast Indian group moved west to **Indian Territory**. Some people from the Seminole, Cherokee, Choctaw, Creek, Catawba, and other **tribes** remained in their traditional homelands east of the Mississippi River.

▲ Southeast Indians celebrate **tribal** history at festivals.

## Southeast Indians today

Today, some Southeast Indian tribes are represented by more than one group. For example, the U.S. government recognizes two different Cherokee groups in Oklahoma and another one in North Carolina. Many **descendants** of Southeast Indians live in cities, suburbs, and small towns all across the United States.

Tribal governments work to provide health care, education, and job opportunities for their people. They also preserve their traditions. At festivals and annual celebrations, Southeast Indians still play stickball and perform traditional dances. Tribes also keep native languages alive by teaching them in schools. Indian leaders know that understanding their past will help them prepare for the future.

### BIOGRAPHY

### Linda Hogan: Chickasaw Writer

Linda Hogan (born 1947) writes poems and stories that reflect her interest in American Indian history and the natural world. She was born in Denver, Colorado, to a Chickasaw father and a white mother. She grew up fascinated by the stories she heard about her Chickasaw **ancestors**. One of the themes of her writing is the link between people and the natural world.

▶ Linda Hogan's writing is based on her American Indian background.

# Timeline

about 10,000 BCE    Humans **migrate** from Asia to North America.

about 9,000 BCE    The first permanent settlements are established in what is now the southeastern United States.

about 2,000 BCE    Ancient Americans begin raising crops.

about 1,000 BCE    Mound-building **cultures** rise in the Southeast.

about 800 CE    Corn becomes a major crop in the Southeast.

1513    Spanish explorer Juan Ponce de León becomes the first European to meet Indians of the Southeast.

1539    Hernando de Soto leads a Spanish **expedition** through the Southeast.

1565    The Spanish establish a settlement at St. Augustine, Florida.

1775–1783    The United States fights for and eventually wins independence during the Revolutionary War, driving European powers from most of the Southeast.

1821    Sequoyah invents a Cherokee written language.

1830    U.S. president Andrew Jackson signs the Indian Removal Act into law.

1831–1839    Cherokee, Chickasaw, Choctaw, Creek, and Seminole peoples are pushed out of their homelands and made to follow the Trail of Tears to **Indian Territory**.

1887    The Dawes Act divides **tribal** lands in Indian Territory.

1907    Oklahoma becomes a state. Indian Territory ceases to exist.

1924    Indians are granted U.S. citizenship under the Indian Citizenship Act.

1934    The Indian Reorganization Act gives Indians the right to practice traditional **ceremonies**.

1968    The American Indian Movement (AIM) organizes protests against the unfair treatment of American Indians and calls on the government to keep its promises to the people.

1978    The American Indian Religious Freedom Act recognizes religion as an important part of Indian life.

1990    Congress passes the Native American Languages Act, "to **preserve**, protect, and promote the rights and freedoms of all Native Americans to use, practice, and develop Native American languages."

1990    President George H. W. Bush proclaims the first National American Indian Heritage Month. President Bill Clinton affirms this special designation in November of 1996.

2004    The National Museum of the American Indian is established on the National Mall in Washington, D.C.

# Glossary

**agriculture** practice of farming or producing crops

**alliance** union between two nations

**ancestor** family member from the distant past

**archaeologist** scientist who studies bones and items left behind by ancient peoples to learn about the past

**breechcloth** garment worn between the legs and tucked over a belt

**cane** thin stem of a woody grass or other plant

**canoe** light, narrow boat

**ceremony** religious event or observance

**chickee** wall-less house on stilts used by the Seminole people of Florida

**chief** leader of a tribe or group of people

**Christianity** religion that follows the beliefs and teachings of Jesus Christ

**clan** group of people who share a common ancestor

**climate** typical weather conditions of a place or region

**culture** shared ways of life and beliefs of a group of people

**culture area** region of North America in which Indians traditionally had a similar way of life

**descendant** offspring of an earlier group

**environment** natural surroundings

**expedition** trip for the purpose of exploration

**fast** to go without eating

**fertile** able to produce plentiful crops

**fertilizer** substance used to make soil more productive

**game** wild animals hunted for food

**geography** science that deals with the location of things on Earth

**Indian Territory** area of present-day Oklahoma once set aside for American Indians

**migrate** move from one place to another

**nation** community of people with its own organization or government

**nomadic** moving from place to place without a fixed home

**nutrient** substance that nourishes

**patchwork** pieces of cloth of various colors and shapes sewn together in a pattern

**plain** broad area of level country

**plaza** public square in a city or town

**sacred** holy or having to do with religious belief

**stockade** wall of posts set up to defend a place

**syllabary** set of written characters, each representing a syllable

**totem** object, such as a plant or animal, that is the emblem of a clan

**treaty** agreement, especially one between two or more countries

**tribal** belonging to a tribe or group of people

**tribe** group of American Indians who share a culture

**wattle and daub** American Indian building style that uses river cane, bark, and vines woven together around poles to form walls

**weir** fence set below water that is used as a trap to catch fish

# Find Out More

## Books

Dennis, Yvonne Wakim, and Arlene Hirschfelder. *A Kid's Guide to Native American History: More Than 50 Activities.* Chicago: Chicago Review, 2010.

Hakim, Joy. *The First Americans.* New York: Oxford, 2005.

King, David C. *First People: An Illustrated History of American Indians.* New York: Dorling Kindersley, 2008.

National Museum of the American Indian. *Do All Indians Live in Tipis?* New York: HarperCollins, 2007.

Sonneborn, Liz. *Wilma Mankiller.* New York: Marshall Cavendish Benchmark, 2010.

## Websites

Cherokee of North Carolina
www.cherokee-nc.com
Learn about the Eastern Band of Cherokee Indians at their official website.

Muscogee (Creek) Nation
www.muscogeenation-nsn.gov/
Learn more about the Muscogee Nation at the group's official website.

PBS's We Shall Remain
www.pbs.org/wgbh/amex/weshallremain/
This is a companion site to the PBS television series, *We Shall Remain*, about the role of American Indians in U.S. history.

Seminole Tribe of Florida
www.seminoletribe.com
Learn about the Seminole tribe of Florida at the group's official website.

## Places to visit

Historical Museum of Southern Florida
101 West Flagler Street
Miami, FL
www.hmsf.org

The Museum of the Native American Resource Center
University of North Carolina at Pembroke
P.O. Box 1510
Pembroke, NC
www.uncp.edu/nativemuseum/

National Museum of the American Indian
Fourth Street and Independence Avenue, SW
Washington, D.C.
www.nmai.si.edu

The Schiele Museum of Natural History
1500 East Garrison Boulevard
Gastonia, NC
www.schielemuseum.org

## Further research

What parts of the Southeast lifestyle did you find the most interesting?
How does life for native peoples in the Southeast compare to the way native
peoples live today in other regions? How did the peoples who first lived in
your area contribute to life today? To learn more about the Southeast or
other culture areas, visit one of the suggested places on these pages or head
to your local library for more information.

# Index